The GREAT FIRE OF LONDON

Written and Illustrated by
Gillian Clements

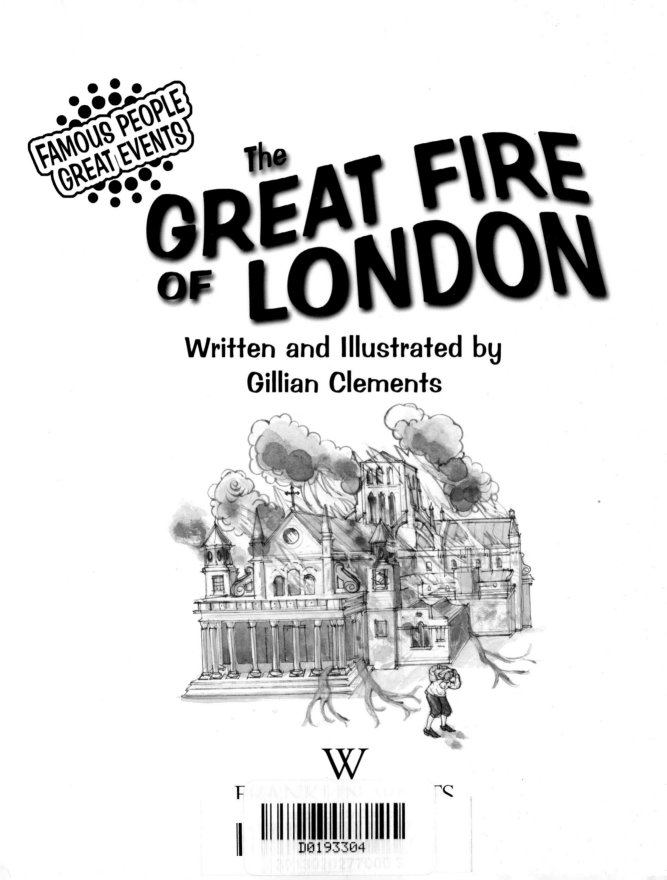

W
F̶R̶A̶N̶K̶L̶I̶N̶ ̶W̶A̶T̶T̶S̶

This edition 2012

Franklin Watts
338 Euston Road
London NW1 3BH

Franklin Watts Australia
Level 17/207 Kent Street
Sydney NSW 2000

Text first published as *Great Events: The Great Fire of London*
in 2001

ISBN: 978 1 4451 0866 7

Dewey Decimal Classification Number: 942.1'066

A CIP catalogue record for this book
is available from the British Library.

Series editor: Sarah Peutrill
Original series editor: Rachel Cooke
Historical consultant: Claire Edwards

Printed in China

Franklin Watts is a division of Hachette Children's Books, an
Hachette UK company.
www.hachette.co.uk

Chapter 1

In 1666 London was already a big city. Half a million people lived there, and it had grown out beyond the old city walls.

The summer of 1666 was very dry.
Londoners were working as usual. But it
was so hot, and the streets were filthy.

Tall wooden houses made the narrow lanes
airless and dark. There was almost no room for
the carts to pass through.

"Oi, look what you're doing!" cried a raker.
"We don't want the plague back this summer!"
   He tried to sweep away sewage, as people
pushed by.

The year before, one hundred
thousand Londoners had died of
the plague.

Rich people like King Charles II and the Lord Mayor had left London. They wanted clean air, and felt safer out of the city.

OXFORD
30 MILES

Chapter 2

Saturday 1st September was another hot, dry day. In Seething Lane by the Tower of London, sat Mr Samuel Pepys, Clerk to the Navy.

Every day he wrote something in his diary – about his work, or life in London. Today he wrote about the danger of the drought.

"Everything is tinder-dry. The Thames is much too low. And there's a strong east wind too. Oh, dear." Pepys was worried. "I must speak to an astrologer," he decided. "I hope Mr Lilly can tell me what will happen."

Few people were about that night. Robbers, known as footpads, hid in the shadows. Children holding lanterns led rich people home safely.

At midnight in Pudding Lane, the baker Thomas Farynor checked his ovens. Then he went upstairs and fell fast asleep. Outside a warm east wind blew clouds of dust across the street.

Chapter 3

Later the baker told his story.

"I woke up choking. It was two o'clock. My maid was coughing and there was smoke everywhere.

That's when I rushed outside... I don't know where my maid is."

An hour later his house was just smoke and ash.

The flames spread. First to the Star
Inn, and then a gust of wind, and
Whoosh! Sparks fell on the warehouses
by the river. The pitch, oil and brandy
inside the buildings made the flames
worse. Thames Street was an inferno.

At his home in Gracechurch Street, the Lord Mayor woke up. He raised his head from the pillow. "Pish! Only a small fire," he yawned and went back to sleep.

Next morning, the east wind was still blowing fiercely. Three hundred houses had burned to the ground. A man shouted, "Fish Street Hill is all on fire!"

Pepys heard the news from his maid. He hurried to the top of the Tower of London to see for himself. "Everything will burn, even the churches! I must tell the King!"

On the way to the Palace at Westminster, Pepys met a lot of angry people. Some thought God had sent the fire. Other people said foreigners living in London had started it.

Pepys just blamed dry weather and a foolish baker.

Pepys found the King at last and told him the dreadful news.

King Charles took command at once, and ordered, "First pull down houses in the fire's path. Then set up fire posts. My brother James will help."

BY ORDER OF THE KING

Make firebreaks. Pull down houses to stop the fire spreading.

Set up fire posts. Organise groups of men to fight the fire.

Get extra soldiers. Call them in from outside London.

Make water pipes. More of them made from elm tree trunks to help carry water to the fire.

But even a King could not hold back a fire like this.

Flames soared thirty metres into the city sky, and the Sun shone red like blood. No one knew how to stop the flames. "There's not enough water in the Thames to put the fire out!"

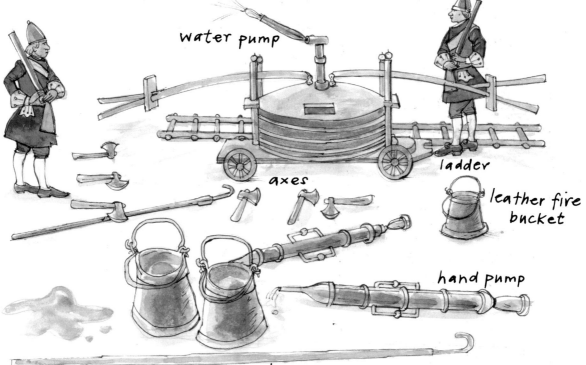

The fires spread west and north.

People stayed in their homes as long as they dared. At the very last moment they fled, in boats called wherries, or on foot.

Lucky carters made a big profit.

Pepys saw terrified pigeons die because "they didn't want to leave their houses. But my wife and I will escape... And I'll come back home tomorrow to bury my wines and cheeses!"

Chapter 4

It was Tuesday now, the third and worst day of the fire. All Cheapside's shops were ablaze and so was Ludgate Hill and Fleet Street. The fire was so hot that even the stones of old St. Paul's were burning.

"Flames are wading through the streets!" said the poet Dryden.

John Evelyn, who also kept a diary at that time, wrote that at night-time: "It was light as day for ten miles round about. Ten thousand houses all in one flame. Melted lead was running down the street."

That lead came from St. Paul's Cathedral. It fell from the roof when sparks lit the timbers. Wall stones exploded and even the pavements below were glowing with heat. The next day St. Paul's Cathedral was a ruin.

By the broken east wall, a schoolboy called Thomas Taswell saw a horrible sight – the body of an old woman, "... her clothes were burnt and every limb reduced to coal."

Everyone feared that the whole city would burn. But the King rode straight to the fire, where he leaped from his horse to grab a firehook. With a quick tug he brought the burning roof thatch down, then he put it out with a bucket of water. People were happy to see their brave King.

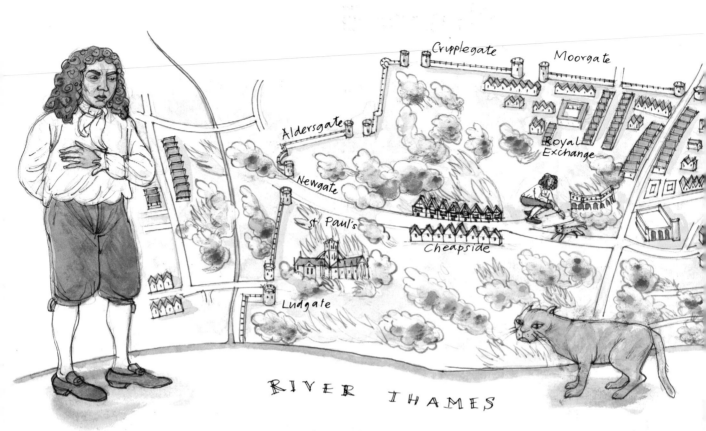

Still the flames spread, north and west to Cripplegate and Fetter Lane.

It made Pepys sad to see the ruins. Hot ashes burned through his shoes.

Near the smoking remains of the Royal Exchange he saw a shivering cat – all its fur burnt off, but still alive.

Chapter 5

But then a miracle happened. The east wind dropped.

Now a breeze blew gently from the north. The fire had come to an end.

Amazingly only six people had died.

The survivors huddled together in Moorfields and Spitalfields. Their sad little bundles held all the belongings they could save from the fire.

"Two hundred thousand people of all ranks and degree in the fields near the city..." wrote Evelyn.

Four-fifths of City burnt
87 churches
13000 houses
44 Company Halls
St. Paul's Cathedral
The Guildhall
Royal Exchange
ALL DESTROYED!

Homes and shops!

Warehouses and halls!

Prisons and sewers!

The King had to act. "We will have an inquiry," he said. "First clear the rubble. Bring these people food and drink, and make them shelters."

Then he looked over the ruins. There was a lot to talk about. How to stop more fires? How to rebuild London? But which first? No one could agree.

24

The King thought, "I want a new, grand city. Build me one like Paris!"

Clever Christopher Wren, the new Surveyor of the King's Works, was just the man to grant Charles his wish.

Wren's London plan was excellent! It was every bit as grand as King Charles had hoped. But the King couldn't afford everything in it. He had spent all his money on a war against France.

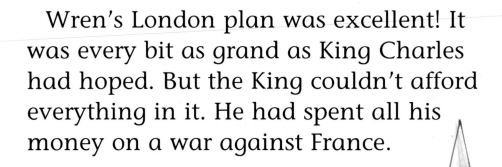

St Paul's
Cathedral

In the end Christopher Wren built 51 new churches, each with a magnificent spire, and a great new domed St. Paul's Cathedral that was finished in 1711.

Every single new building had to be made of brick and stone, because wood burned too easily.

27

After the fire there were other new 'Regulations' to follow.

The City set up fire brigades. People were careful to sweep up their rubbish. And, unlike the baker Thomas Farynor, everyone made their household ashes safe at night!

It took 10 years and more than seven million pounds to rebuild London.

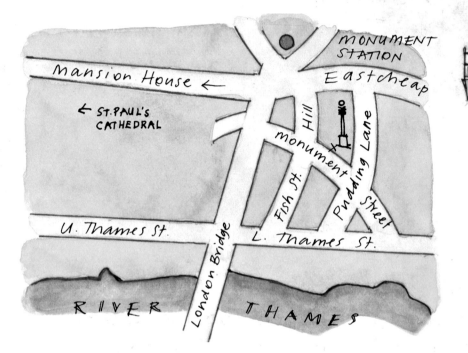

Today if you go to London, you might like to visit St. Paul's – or the Monument. Christopher Wren built that too, and it stands near Pudding Lane where the Great Fire began.

Timeline

1561 St. Paul's Cathedral is struck by lightning. Timber spire burns away.

1603 Bubonic plague kills 30,000 people in London.

1616 William Shakespeare dies.

1632 Christopher Wren is born.

1633 Samuel Pepys is born.

1642 English Civil War begins.

1649 Charles I (Charles II's father) is executed. The 'Commonwealth' begins under Oliver Cromwell.

1660 Pepys begins to keep his diary.
The Restoration: England has a king again – King Charles II.

1661 John Evelyn criticises London's air pollution.

1665 Isaac Newton experiments with gravity.
Summer: The Great Plague strikes London. Many people, including King Charles, leave the city.

1666 February: King Charles returns to London.

1666 2nd–5th September: the Great Fire of London.

11th September: Wren presents his plans for rebuilding London.

25th September: Fire Inquiry begins.

1667 The Rebuilding Act sets out laws on how to rebuild London.

1669 Wren is appointed Surveyor of the King's Works. Pepys, worried about his eyesight, stops keeping his diary.

1675 Rebuilding of St. Paul's Cathedral begins.

1685 Charles II dies. His brother James II becomes king.

1686 Wren's 51 churches completed.

1689 James II is replaced by his sister Mary and her husband, William of Orange.

1703 Samuel Pepys dies.

1711 St. Paul's Cathedral is completed.

1723 Wren dies, aged 91.

Quiz

Can you remember?

1. In what year did the Great Fire of London happen?

2. How many people were living in London at the time?

3. Where did the fire start?

4. Who told the King about the Great Fire?

5. What was on fire that the king himself put out?

6. What stopped the fire?

7. Where did the people who had lost their homes go?

8. How many people died in the fire?

9. Who made the plans for rebuilding London?

10. How long did it take to rebuild London after the fire?

Answers on page 32

Glossary

all ranks and degree Every kind of person, including rich and poor.

astrologer A person who studies the stars and planets to try to see into the future.

diary A written record of daily events.

firehook A hook on the end of a long stick used to move burning material.

inquiry A special investigation set up to find out why something has happened.

John Evelyn Scholar, writer and diarist who lived in the 17th century.

lead A type of metal that was used a lot in the past in the roofs and windows of buildings.

plague Deadly disease caught by humans from rat-fleas.

raker A street cleaner.

regulations Rules.

sewage Sludgy, dirty waste, mainly from baths and toilets. Sewage used to be thrown out of houses into open channels in the street.

Index

Quiz answers

1. 1666
2. Half a million
3. In a baker's house in Pudding Lane
4. Samuel Pepys
5. A roof
6. The wind coming from the north instead of the east
7. To the fields around London (Moorfields and Spitalfields)
8. 6
9. Christopher Wren
10. Ten years